To Sarah and Mark,

Your godfather told me about your wonderful courtship and upcoming wedding.

May your lives be graced with harmony and may you enjoy the kind of enduring, generous love that this book celebrates.

Deborah Hearing Khayat

Gathered Blooms

ISBN 0-9748730-7-1
First Edition

Gathered Blooms

A Celebration of Love in Verse Form

———◆·×·◆———

Written and Illustrated by
Deborah Dearing Khayat

Westview Publishing, Inc., Nashville, Tennessee

To all who have known love and were warmed by its ardor, assured by its endurance, comforted by its compassion, enriched by its generosity, awed by its capacity, and marvel at its mystery.

Contents

The Bouquet

Does love transcend all poetry,
Or are there words to find
That will capture all it is
In accent, meter, rhyme?

If such be true, then I shall try
To replace the poorer prose
With bouquets of these fragrant words —
No thorns, but just the rose.

To you I'll give these gathered blooms
Arranged so you can see
Just what the magic of your love
Truly means to me.

I pray these fervent offerings
Won't wither or grow old.
Please keep the memory of them
Pressed deep within your soul.

The Cache

Passion comes. It doth insist
    Lie with me, we can't resist
Apparent glories. But, wait! There's more
    That's hid behind sequestered doors.
Take time to find each hidden treasure,
    Then linger there – exquisite pleasure.

Apart

Dappled sunshine falls upon the pillow bare,
And waking lets me know that you're not there.
'Twas dreams of you that kept the truth at bay.
I know that now, in solitude of day.

Would that dreams pervade the waking hours
As dew alights and clings to morning's flowers.
Then to be with you might ne'er be done
And reverie would best the new day's sun.

Together

'Tis true, you're here — we have the chance
    To set the dreams aside.
We're in the realm of real romance —
    Together, you and I.

Now that sweet imagining
    Is in a place that's past,
Our hearts entwined can finally sing —
    Oh, ecstasy at last.

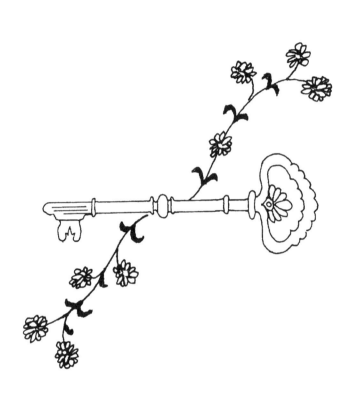

Did You Know?

You live in the quiet places of my mind.
 I have the only key,
And when I choose to visit there,
 Delicious reverie.

All the senses locked inside
 Now ready to be free —
Touch and taste and sight and sound;
 Renewed intensity.

Did you know you lived elsewhere?
 That you reside in me?
No other boarder shares this space —
 Sweet exclusivity.

The Invitation

My heart doth bid you, Enter please.
Come through this open Door,
And once inside, Beloved Guest,
Stay here, forevermore.

The Birthday

It's not just yours to celebrate,
  I share the day with thee –
For that first one, it was the start
  On your way to me.

As the passing years were feted,
  The candles lit, then blown –
You were coming ever closer
  To a love as yet unknown.

And then the crossroads happened.
  The passion, oh, so rife.
I know it now for what it was –
  The birthday of MY life.

To My Dearest Love

When shall we meet again?
I hope the wait's not long...
Though time could never dull the sound
Of you, my life's sweet song.

Our Voice

You are my Robert Browning,
  Elizabeth am I.
We write of love and longing –
  In verses does this lie.

A Providential Planner
  Gave to you and me
Words the Angels must have kissed –
  A voice called Poetry.

Were I With You . . .

Your hands I'd kiss for in their touch
    Is found a sweet caress
That gives to me a cherished gift —
    Unrivaled tenderness.

Your eyes I'd kiss for what I see
    Reflected in their shine.
What it is envelops me —
    A loving gaze sublime.

Your lips I'd kiss for from them come
    Such words I must secrete
And keep them safe, for only they,
    Can give my heart its beat.

And if I would beside you lie
    And rest beneath love's cover,
I'd give this heart that lives for you
    And love you like no other.

The Visitor

When Love stopped by to see me,
I was not yet prepared.
No table set in silver,
No flowers in my hair.

It came right in and stayed with me
As though it weren't a guest,
And made itself a happy home,
No need for Sunday best.

The Captive

I lie awake and think of you,
And when dreams come, you're in them too.
Imprisoned by these thoughts sublime,
I can't escape this cell divine;
Nor do I wish to be set free,
But rather choose eternity.

My Paradox

You are my precious paradox –
A puzzlement profound.
But gratitude resounds in me
That I to this am bound:

You're the reason that I breathe.
You give me life each day;
Yet with impassioned ardency,
You take my breath away.

The Banquet

Come to me, Beloved.
    It's time for our embrace;
The fruits of love hang heavy —
    O Gardener, make haste.

Don't let this bounty wither
    Or perish on the vine;
It waits to give you pleasure —
    O Harvester, it's time.

And when this Banquet's ended,
    With hunger gone, 'tis true,
The table is not empty —
    There's always food anew.

For planting never ceases
    As seasons come and go,
Fresh seeds forever scattered,
    O Sower, make Love grow.

The Request

You took me on a voyage
    To a place I'd never been.
Will you, dear Charter of that Course,
    Please take me there again?

When can we book such passage?
    Oh, wait be not too long
To visit past remembrances
    Of love's eternal song.

The Cure

Today I'm feeling saddened
   Because you're far from me.
I need to find a cure for this —
   A perfect remedy.

I'll make a magic potion
   To chase away these blues;
Every symptom will be banished,
   And all because of you.

I'll think of all that you possess
   And what I can conscript —
To make this panacea a
   Success I can predict.

All the wonders that are you —
   What sets you far apart,
I'll take the memory of them
   And soothe my aching heart.

Raiment

Night is here
  And darkened shadows cloak me,
Though soon I'll wear a
  Dress of lighter hue.
Dreams of love
  Will banish all the darkness,
And I'll be swathed
  In the brightness of you.

Morning's come and dreams are done.
  I shall be garbed anew.
Now in all my daylight hours,
  I'm clothed in the sunshine of you.

A Solitary Tear

A solitary tear,
    That falls from saddened eyes,
Harbors no insistence
    To stop and rest awhile;
But rather keeps on going,
    And lonely though it be,
It has no wish to wait for
    More doleful company.

My Song

My song had not yet started.
  The notes could not be sung;
But now that you are here with me,
  Life's melody's begun.

My song will rise to Heaven,
  Resplendent in its sound,
A hymn exalting what we are —
  One voice, forever bound.

My song resounds in dual tones.
  This chorus is its power;
And now with voices joined as one,
  It's not just mine, but ours.

Another Day

My heart grows restless in the wait.
I pray the sun will not be late;
For when its roseate strains arrive,
I'll know the heavens did contrive
To give what is the world to me —
Another day of loving thee.

Let Me Stay a Little Longer

Let me stay a little longer
    In the warmth of your embrace.
I am a happy captive
    In this most cherished place.

Let me stay a little longer
    To see more lovelight shine.
It's here and most abundant
    When your eyes look into mine.

Let me stay a little longer,
    Or I would surely miss
One more chance to revel in
    The passion of your kiss.

Let me stay a little longer,
    With each moment grows anew
The rapture of the ceaseless love
    That I would give to you.

Supersedere

O glorious orb hung low in the sky,
    What silvery fullness dazzles the eye!
Stargazers revel in sated delight,
    As stark luminescence charges the night.

Yet, there is something can pale this tableau
    And dim the candescence of its fulgent glow.
All that thou art, and the face that I see,
    Will cause it to temper in deference to thee.

The Blessing

I take my leave; now time will wax forlorn
'Til tender recollections, newly born,
Assuage this fated farewell's sorrowed sting-
Blessed is the nectar of remembering.

Your Love

Your love is like an island shore.
    It wraps the whole of me,
And with each wave that touches land,
    I am caressed by thee.

Your love is like the island tide
    Returning faithfully;
And with each day, as dawn arrives,
    I feel your constancy.

Restitution

We lost another hour,
I wonder where it went,
This victim of some circumstance
We, sadly, couldn't prevent.

Hours stolen from our love
Should get a dispensation,
But if not, there's still a chance
For proper compensation.

I hope someone is finding them —
That they're not thrown away,
And when they number twenty-four,
We're given back a day.

Where Did It Lie?

Where did it lie, secluded, unshown,
While whispering truths were unheard and unknown?

Was it there in the hallway of forthcoming dreams
Behind a closed door seeping untethered beams?

Somewhere Love waited, its power accrued,
And would not be witnessed until there was you.

The Morning

I wake to greet the morning.
    Alas, you are not here.
I cannot feel the warmth of you
    Or touch your face so dear.

I wake to greet the morning
    And weep that you're away,
But love had crossed the wide divide
    And found me where I lay.

I wake to greet the morning;
    I rise, now not alone,
For always you shall dwell with me,
    My heart – your joyous home.

At First Glance

Beloved you were, right from the start,
  Those feelings written in my heart;
And at first glance, I could predict –
  Indelible would be the script.
Sweet ink, it ne'er will fade away,
  And with that truth I live today.

Silence of the Heart

There's a silence of the heart that we as lovers hear,
The rest between the beats resounds astonishingly clear.
This rhythmic, subtle stillness, perceived with little strife,
Renews the vigor and sustains the music of our life.

Harmony

Robin red and Purple Grackle
    Flew from the sky in twos,
And shared the space upon the ground
    With Yellow-Billed Cuckoos.
All their purpose very firm —
To seek the lowly, lovely worm.

Then a Sparrow, fresh from flight,
Joined the Nuthatch, breasted white.
Next a Kinglet, ruby crowned,
He by no restriction bound,
Entered this most friendly spree
With a Black-Capped Chickadee.

As each they tried their food to find,
And though they were of different kind,
Their feathers rested in contentment —
No interest shown in such resentment.

If only people that diverse,
Those who share this universe,
    Could similarly be
Vested in the raiment of
    Compatibility.

Take My Hand

Take my hand and take my heart
      And at unhurried pace,
We'll walk together down a road
      With all travail erased.
We'll find no sadness in a tear,
      No terror in the night,
No loneliness in solitude,
      No dark without the light.
The days will be resplendent in
      The promises we'll keep;
Communion everlasting is
      the benediction reaped.

The Net

You talk to me and speak of love.
    It floats on dulcet air;
Now echoes of these sweetest sounds
    Reverberate somewhere.

If only I could cast a net
    And catch what flies so free,
So all the essence of your words
    Would then belong to me.

No Earthly Measure

Motion, force and space and time
Can all be measured, sure and fine;
But there's nothing we can do
To measure love, sublime and true.
No instrument can quantify,
No gauge determines depth or size.

My love of you resists all bounds,
The borders known, it just confounds.
This heart is not content to be
The keeper of its equity;
So all the love I have for you
Repels constraints and courses through
Every aspect of my being,
Infinite the joy it's bringing.

There is no earthly way to measure
This love of you, my dearest treasure;
But Heaven might, if we insist,
Find a paradigm for this.

Our Prayer

As we begin this time of living
    Together joined as one,
May our joy be unabated
    And sadness never come.

As we begin this time of giving
    To each other without fail,
May our hearts replete with kindness
    Be constant and prevail.

As we begin this time of caring
    For such needs that may arise,
May we always see the comfort
    In each other's eyes.

As we begin this time of loving
    Of our souls' captive mate,
May a love that binds with strongest ties
    Now be our joyous fate.

A Gift

It's still the morning of my love;
    There is no close of day.
I've never traveled to a place
    Where evening shadows stray.

Though years have passed between us,
    Their number is not true,
For days that have no endings
    Cannot be counted new.

There's ever something yet to find,
    A quality then cherished,
Which makes me love you even more,
    And leaves me dearly nourished.

All these fresh awakenings
    Resist the thief of time,
Sentries halting twilight's march
    Allowing this design.

Ceaseless riches to discover,
    I think I always knew,
They are a present just for me,
    A gift, for loving you.

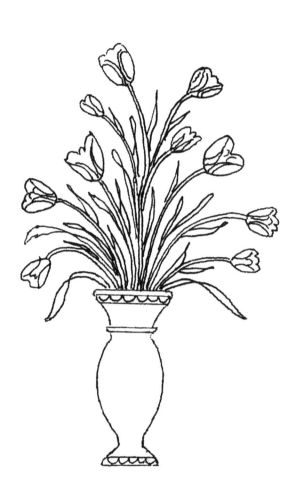

I Shall Not Bid Adieu

I loved you in the spring of youth
    With beauty's flower unfurled;
And now in winter's frosty grasp,
    With petals dropped and curled,
It matters not the season's sting —
    I shall not bid adieu.
The precious fragrance of your being
    No climate can subdue.

The Director

How does it really happen?
Should we look above?
Heaven maybe can explain
The wonder that is Love.

Does God prepare a script for us,
Then cast us in our parts,
And if we're faithful to His plan,
We'll find each other's heart?

If so, I'm glad we did not stray
From what He'd always planned –
That we should be, the two of us,
Forever hand in hand.

More

I reach into the silence to find past words of love,
And in the quiet vastness, beside me and above,
I hear those gentle whispers, embrace the tender sighs,
Then yearn to see that love for me reflected in your eyes.

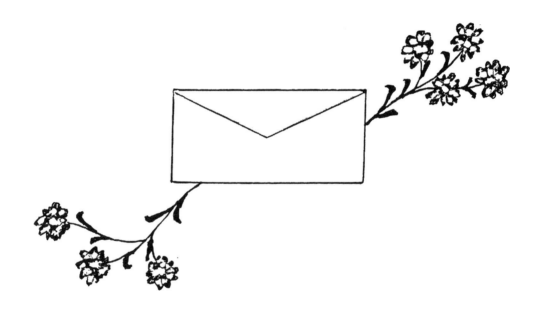

The Envelope

Resting in the envelope of time,
Long lying in the shadows of my mind,
Are images of love and how it grew
When blessed fate gave me the gift of you.
And always they are clear and have remained
Unaltered and impervious, unchanged.

I'll Meet You There

I'll meet you there, Beloved,
    In the place that's yours and mine.
It's beyond a far horizon,
    Where the bell of truth will chime.

It sounds in celebration,
    As it has year after year,
Of love's enduring presence –
    And only we can hear.

There hidden from all worldly view,
    Known but to you and me,
This haven for our minds' caress –
    We cherish steadfastly.

I'll meet you there, Beloved,
    In the place that's yours and mine,
Where love lies moored and ready
    To refuse the tides of time.

The Stage

The conscious curtain rises,
  Proscenium laid bare,
Preparing for my play of life's
  Reprised performance there.

My mind's eye sees the plot unfold –
The cast, regrouped, appears.
Upon this stage unraveled is
The labyrinth of years.

Now as the curtain falls in close,
  Yet waits again to rise,
I know with certainty I saw
  Repeated truth survive.

Of all the players in each scene
  Presented for review,
The one commanding center stage
  Is still and only – you.

Do Not Weep

Do not weep, O dearest darling,
When my life surrenders sound;
For my heart's song shall not be silenced,
But will then in you be found.

This voice will not be ended,
Nor its quality diminished,
But will begin again in you
And greet a finer finish.

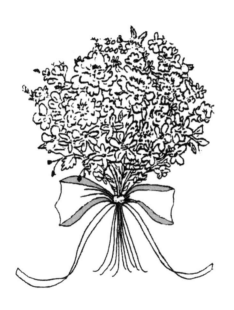